THE LOVER'S RHAPSODY

ECSTATIC LOVE POEMS OF RAPTURE, AWAKENING, AND GOD

ADAM MALIK SIDDIQ

Copyright © 2020 by Adam Malik Siddiq.
All rights reserved.

No part of this book may be reproduced in any form or by any electronic or mechanical means, including information storage and retrieval systems, without written permission from the author, except for the use of brief quotations in a book review.

For information about this title or to order other books and/or electronic media, contact the publisher:

LINEAGE PUBLISHING
1201 S. Los Angeles Street #2,
Los Angeles, CA 90015
www.lineagepublishing.com
info@lineagepublishing.com

ISBN: 978-1-946852-03-8

Printed in the United States of America.

First and foremost, I dedicate this collection of poems to the Spirit of Love… the Universal Soul… God.

Secondly, with great humility and honor, I pay respect and tribute to my great guides, Mawlānā Jalāl ad-Dīn Muhammad Balkhī, Shams-i-Tabrīzī, Khwāja Shams-ud-Dīn Muḥammad Ḥāfeẓ, Saadi Shirazi, and my grandfather, Khaled Siddiq Charkhi.

Thirdly, I dedicate this work to my entire family for all the love they poured into me and our environment, especially my grandparents, mother Tooba and father Siddiq, brother Abeal, and sisters Eve and Fati.

Fourthly, I pray this work will bless my future generations with the love beyond loves and honor my ancestors with my devotion to serve, lead, and inspire others with the gifts I'm here to give.

Finally, I dedicate all the love, all the passion, all the joy, all the celebration, all the heart, all the energy, all the magic of life I poured and allowed pour through me to create this poetic compilation to all of humanity.

Without Love, we are nothing. With Love, we are beyond any-thing.

Contents

A Note From The Author ix
Foreword xi

The Lover's Rhapsody 1
I Am A Sailboat 4
All I See Is Your Face 5
The Oasis That Never Runs Dry 6
Giver Of All, Taker Of None! 8
Every Day Is A Holy-day 9
What Am I To Do In This Mad World? 10
Enough With These Silly Remarks! 13
Praise Be To This Incompleteness! 15
Where Does A Tree Begin? Where Does A Tree End? 17
By The Grace Of Love! 20
Beyond Sense And Nonsense 22
Enough With The Parrot Talk! 23
The Lover Of Love 24
I've Searched For You 27
Everything You Give 28
In Your Dreaming 30
Oh Great Heart! 32
Oh Great Guardian Of Love! 34
Where Are You From? 35
Teach Me How To Live 37
The Loudest Sound 39
Love's Prayer Rug 40
Humanity's Prayer And Answering 41
As I Pray 42

Seen, Unseen, Heard, Unheard	44
Enough?	46
The Lover's Entire Being	48
Surrender To Joy	49
Inhale…Exhale…	50
The Addiction Of Truth	52
Hurricane Of Love	53
There Is A Sweetness Beyond Sweetness	54
What Good Is A Heart Without Love?	56
The Myth Of Sensitivity	58
The Kiss That Blows Existence	60
The Special Friendship	63
The Mystic, The Cup, The Wine	65
Love's Rain	67
How You Answer The Call	68
Diversity	70
This Fragrance	73
Finding Treasure	75
Ever Since I Was Created	77
Heartbreak Or Heartwake?	78
Love's Fermentation	79
You Are The Promise Fulfilling	81
Being Purpose	82
No Sleep For The Soul	84
The Placeless Place	86
Breathe Like A Lover	88
Pour Yourself Through Myself	90
Who? What? Why?	94
The Gift Of Potential	96
Dark Night Of The Soul	98
The Balm	100
Oh God! Where Are You?	102
Even The Smallest Spark	104
Forget Mindfulness	105
Eyes Of Infinity	106

A Special Relationship	107
Beloved's Alchemy	109
Who Is This Friend?	111
The Frog And The Pond	113
Sweet Silence	115
The Vagabond	116
Hope And Faith	117
O Sweet Gratitude!	119
Dancing Like Incense Smoke	120
What Keeps You Up At Night	122
A City In Ruins	124
The Womb	125
A Tribute To Mothers	126
Lost	127
A Message To People Pleasers	128
Love Has Made Me A Madman	129
Between Future And Past	130
The Visionary	132
The Lover's Insanity	133
What Are You Seeking?	134
Because It Was You	135
Soul Has Taken Me	136
Love Is Wild	137
Nectar Of Life	138
The Roof Has Collapsed From Within	139
Who Is It That Seeks Within My Seeking?	140
Burning In Love	141
Lion Of Love	142
Come, Come, My Dear Heart	143
Witness As A Lover	144
Love's Passion To Serve	145
Explore With Passion	146
Drunk In My Longing	147
Blessed By The Burning Of Love	148
Remembering And Forgetting	149

Rubab Of Joy 150
Afterlife 151
Bonus Verses 153

A Note From The Author

Dear reader,

The Lover's Rhapsody is a collection of poems written all around the world, at sacred sites, ancient and underground cities, majestic natural wonders, and throughout visits at the shrines of saints like Mawlānā Jalāl ad-Dīn Muhammad Balkhī ("Rumi") and Shams-i-Tabrīzī.

Every poem was written during the experience of spiritual states and mystical trances.

You may notice a certain poem or a specific verse that speaks so deeply to your soul that you seem to be taken somewhere else, and you may feel overcome with an overwhelming amount of energy.

When you feel this, allow yourself the time and space to fully be with your experience.

Each poem is a spiritual transmission that's intended to be felt deeply while you're reading.

Revisit these transmissions over time and you'll find new depth in each verse.

My intention is that these poems awaken you to the beauty and depth of your true nature as a soul, as well as inspire you to expand your devotional service in showing up to life as a being of Love.

Love,
Adam Malik Siddiq

P.S. If you feel compelled to share your experiences of reading *The Lover's Rhapsody* with me, find me on Facebook and Instagram @TheAdamSiddiq. I love reading your stories!

Foreword

I had the honor and pleasure of reading the *The Lover's Rhapsody* by Adam Siddiq. I congratulate Adam on his excellent work of literature. When I read these poems, it was evident to me that Adam is a passionate, devoted follower of Mawlānā Jalāl ad-Dīn Muhammad Balkhī. Like Mawlānā, Adam's poems are infused with love. On the topic of love, I have several insightful perspectives to share from some of the greatest mystical poets of all time.

First, Mawlānā Jalāl ad-Dīn Muhammad Balkhī says:

"Love is my master.
Knowledge is my servant."

Mawlānā said that when God created the universe, God fell in love with the universe and the universe fell in love with God. As a result, love is God and love is the essence that unifies all existence.

Second, there is Khwāja Shams-ud-Dīn Muḥammad Ḥāfeẓ who says:

"In the beginning, when the ray of God's light flashed,
Love made a fire in the earth and from this came man."

And…

"O beautiful wine-bearer, bring forth the cup and put it to my lips.
The path of love seemed easy at first, what came was many hardships."

Third, Saib Tabrizi says:

"Love took everything from me: my heart, religion, and knowledge.

Now, how can I get back what I have lost?"

Fourth, Sheikh Saadi Shirazi says:

"When love comes inside you,
love will take everything from inside you.
Your patience, quietness, and heart will be taken."

Let me not forget that Abul-Ma'ālī Mīrzā Abdul-Qādir Bēdil, who is immersed in the love of God, says:

"However you bend your head in *sajda*,
when you meet God,
you must do it one hundred-thousand times with all your love."

Anyone who has been taken over by love in the ways these mystical poets have spoken about has done the job. I have also written a poem in Dari (Farsi), which in English goes something as follows:

When the radiance of love shined in the universe,
all lovers were lost in love.

When the song of the reed flute was played,
all colors, fragrances, and nuisances of life became vibrant in the garden of love.

Love is music,
Music is love.
You can't escape the prison of love.

Love is faith,
Love is culture,
Love is religion.
All is recorded in the manuscript of love.

When the love of God shined upon the universe,
the entire universe became the glimmering reflection of love.

Love does not belong to you or me.
The belief of love is free from all thoughts.

Love is burning, madness, and chasing.
Everyone with a heart is clinging onto love with their life.

Love is humble, gentle, and kind.
Self-importance and pride are not in the conscience of love.

Overall, I desire for Adam Siddiq to have another great success with this book and for his pen to always get sharper.

Warmly,
Khaled Siddiq Charkhi

The Lover's Rhapsody

Lovers pitch tents under the stars
and stay up all night
rhapsodizing in awe
about the Soul of the Universe.

One lover begins their tale,
"This Mysterious Presence,
this Illuminating Essence,
lifts my soul with Transcendence!
All illusions
dissipate into the Light.
All that's real
shines so bright!"

Another lover shares their tale,
"The Miracle Maker,
the Heart's Waker,
Love's Caretaker,
the Cosmic Matchmaker,
whispered to my soul
a million love poems
in one silent breath.
Ever since,
I remain wakeful,
ever-present,
in my patient waiting,
ever-yearning,
for another moment
of Love's euphoric kiss."

A third lover shares their tale,
"I used to look above
from below
feeling so separate
from all I wish to know,
until…
one night,
as I stared into the moonlight,
the moon whispered to my heart,

'The brilliance you seek
is what you are.'

My timid soul
asked the moon,

'Dear moon,
how do you know this to be true?
You hover above
and shine such beautiful light
on all of us below.
Your brilliance is beyond
anything I can ever imagine to be
and anything I can ever aspire to be.
I am nothing.
You are something phenomenal.'

The moon smiled.
'Dear soul,
is it not my light.
It is not my brilliance.
I am only a reflection
of the Brilliance
that you are.
I am only a reflection

of the Light
that you are.
You are no-thing.
You are the Delight
that makes the galaxies swirl.
You are the Infatuation
that inspires the cosmos
to passionately manifest
chaos into order…
some-thing
from no-thing.'

The moonlight filled
the windows of my mind
and I lost my-self.
Doubts turned to smiles,
fears turned to joys,
as I became the Celestial Tune
that makes constellations
sing as One."

I Am A Sailboat

I am a sailboat rocking
in the Winds of Love,
exploring the Sea of Consciousness.
I am a fruit tree growing
in the Garden of Life,
blooming with Ardour.
I am a cup of chai brewing
within the Pot of Divinity,
burning with Passion.
I am a pebble thrown
in the Ocean Of Bliss,
sinking into multi-dimensional Love.
I am heart-filled laughter
in the field of Expansive Joy,
echoing with intoxicating admiration for the One.
Like honey made of Love's Sweetness,
my loving never expires for my Beloved.
My every doing,
My very being
is a rhapsody for Love.

All I See Is Your Face

I'm tormented with passion.
All I see is Your Face.
I'm intoxicated with desire.
All I see is Your Face.
I'm growling with hunger.
All I see is Your Face.
I'm sleepless with longing.
All I see is Your Face.
I'm aching with fervidness.
All I see is Your Face.
I'm bewildered with myself.
All I see is Your Face.

The Oasis That Never Runs Dry

While many bask in the mirages of this world,
lovers wander crazily throughout the vast deserts of emptiness
with a thirst beyond thirsts
for this Oasis that springs with Majesty
and never runs dry.

They leave everything behind
in their fervid longing for their Beloved.
They give of themselves entirely
for the loving of such Profundity.
Their hearts grow feverish
and ache for more,
every step of the way,
and then sweetness pours through
and the madness of love ensues.
Such an ache is not painful;
It is pure invigoration.

These love-drunkards are guided through nothingness
with such precise accuracy.
Their compass: their hearts.
The direction they're led:
into the Heart of hearts.

With one sip,
they rise in frenzied jubilation,
their whole-beings singing,
"Oh Love!

That which makes me rise in Eternity's Rapture
and set within Joy's Pasture!
You have given me sweetness
beyond sensations.
You have granted me refuge
within the Heart of hearts,
where all is One,
where all is Love,
and yet,
I crave You like the shore craves to be washed,
wave after wave,
by the Ocean,
always and forever."

Such a love story brings one to their knees
with humbling gratitude for the Giver of gifts.

Giver Of All, Taker Of None!

Oh Life!
How You bring me into one e-motion
and then into another!
How You raise me with experiences!
How You bless me with lividness
and then laughter!
How You strengthen me with courage
and then caress me with rapture!
How You sculpt me with might
and then melt me with love!
How You course through me vigorously
and then lift me into blissful no-thing-ness!

Oh Life!
Giver of all!
Taker of none!
One kiss from Your Lips has ripped me open from myself!
You've torn off the mask
and given me a mirror,
in it Your Face.

Every Day Is A Holy-day

Oh Love!
Because of You,
I have become intoxicated with Reality.
I now see that every day is a holy-day.
I now feel that every moment is a holy-moment.
I now know that between every-every and every-none,
within moments and across days,
beyond time and beneath space,
there is a Sea of Holiness
from which Life pours into life.

Oh Love!
Your Kiss has freed me
from the shackles of time.
Now I am a free spirit
celebrating all as Divinity
throughout all of Eternity.

What Am I To Do In This Mad World?

Oh Love!
What am I to do in this mad world
where the major sources of information
are ridden with fear, hatred, deceit, and corruption;
where brands and advertisers want to sell me to be
everything except for my own unique self;
where bigotry gets the spotlight over kindness;
where nature has become known as the alternative;
where news divide us into two opposing directions
and says what it says through the ventriloquists,
with talks about mindless politics and obsessive profitability,
as opposed to the voices of Truth and Love?

Dear soul!
You are of the Major Source of Information.
Love is what has made you in-form-ation!
Only the spiritually blind want to live in a world of fear.
Only the spiritually numb want to live in a world of hate.
Wake people up to their spiritual senses!
Ignite the heart-threads of any of the many
with Love's Presence as your torch
and watch the Love-Flame kindle throughout the field,
like a wildfire of Life waking up to its Sacred Nature.
Knowing oneself is a freedom of its own.
Knowing your nature is knowing Nature.
Truth is what liberates
and as you are liberated by the Truth of your nature,
so are others.

All those shadows can no longer pretend to be
the big, bad, unstoppable monsters they want to be
when faced with the light of Truth.
Not even all the illusions stand a chance to exist
in the presence of one enlightened candle.
Imagine what's possible with many!
Your realization has cleared the way
for your purposeful task.
Be one with Love and you will become the Love the world needs.

A tree has many purposes.
One of which is to plant more trees.
However, you don't see the tree picking off its own fruit,
tearing away to their centers to pluck out its own seeds.
Nor do you see it planting those seed,
nor watering them.
All the tree does is exist as its unique self.
From there, its own natural rhythm is in sync with the Rhythm of Life.
The Rhythm of Life is what calls all the necessary expressions of Life to
and from the tree to serve its sacred purpose in creating more abundance.
When the tree's fruit has reached a state of ripeness,
some beings will eat the fruit,
others break the twigs to make a nest,
some fruit fall to the ground where insects pick away at it,
and surely,
the fruit's seeds are left to sink into the ground.
The wind scatters them across the earth
and the rain and soil nourishes them
with its essential needs.
Then comes spring and the tree wears fresh new garments of green,
all while its seeds have sprouted with new life,
fulfilling the promises invested within them.

Be like a tree that's in love with Love,
that's alive with Life,

that brings life to Life.
All that you are to do is to be that which you naturally are.
Be yourself passionately.
Share your gifts passionately.
This is the way of life.

Enough With These Silly Remarks!

Enough with these silly remarks
of "best" and "most",
and "greatest" and "number one",
and "top three" and "ultimate",
and "highest" and "lowest".
Love does not see in these terms.

Enough with the incessant hunger
to be the "best",
to be "right",
to prove the others "wrong",
to see everyone you meet
as another competitor that you must "beat"…
be it by your proclaimed accomplishments,
the status you hold in society,
your material possessions,
the clothes and jewelry you're wearing,
and whatever other shenanigans this material matrix
has taught you to identify yourself with.
Love does not see in these terms.

Enough with this cloud of anxiety,
the lizard brain's whispering-shoutings.
These voices that have haunted you in your steps for far too long
are not even your own.
"Will there be enough?"
"Is there enough?"
"Do I have enough?"

"Am I enough?"
Think of what you are!
Think of what you're made of!
Think of where you come from!
You are the product of Love,
and Love only makes miraculous magnificence.
Is Love "enough"?
Love is beyond words,
beyond thoughts,
beyond the most admired thing of this material world.
Love is what brings all together.
Love is what we are.
Be that essence which you are and witness treasures unfold
like a monsoon after a long drought.
Where you once worried there was scarcity,
Love springs an oasis from the ground.

Love is your beginning and your end.
Love is your Source.
Let Love be the reason of your every doing,
simply by being.
And from being,
a spring of Joy emerges.
Be a lighthouse.
Call souls back Home with the Effulgence
that has sparked our very existence.
That is our very existence.

Praise Be To This Incompleteness!

Praise be to this incompleteness,
this engulfing sense that
I am not enough for the awakening
that I wish to see for all beings of this world,
for it is this incompleteness that gifts hunger.

Praise be to this grumbling hunger
that reverberates throughout my being
and haunts my every waking moment,
fixating my focus and guiding me
with instinct and intuition
to collaborate,
participate,
share,
receive,
bless,
and be,
wherever,
however,
and with whomever
this Tailor of Love guides the union
of Love's soul-threaded creations together,
weaving a Tapestry of Majesty,
for it is this hunger that gifts the seeking.

Praise be to this fervid seeking,
this passionate longing
that echoes of the song

between the lover and the Beloved,
for it is this seeking that gifts the Knowing.

Praise be to this Knowing,
this Eternal Presence,
this Brilliant Truth that pierces all veils
between "you" and "me",
between "lover" and "Beloved",
allowing realized experiencing of
the Heart of hearts,
the Cosmic Harmony,
the Sea of Love,
the Oneness,
the Every-ness,
the Infiniteness,
for this Knowing is Home.

Where Does A Tree Begin?
Where Does A Tree End?

Where does a tree begin?
Where does a tree end?
Is it just the structure
of roots, trunk, branches, leaves, flowers, and fruit?
Is it also the nests that the birds have crafted upon its branches
and the music they make?
Is it also the colonies of insects that walk upon it?
Is it also the seed it once was?
Is it also the fruit from which that seed came from?
Is it also still part of the tree from which the fruit
from which the seed it once was came from?
And how about the fruit that contained the seed from which that tree
came from?
Which tree is its true origin?

Is it still the seed,
ever-expanding,
ever-unfolding,
ever-growing?
Is it also part of those trees that grow
from the seeds of its fallen fruits?
Or has the tree ended there
where new separate-seeming ones begin?
Does it end once the fruit has fallen?
And what about the fallen leaves and branches?
Are they still part of the tree?
Does a tree end where the edge of its shade ends?

Does it end beyond its tallest branch and leaves?
Or perhaps when the bees come to pollinate,
is the pollen received by the bees from the tree no longer part of it?
Or does the tree continue to live on from what the bees carry?

Trees, like life, are not prisoners of time.
They are not bound by space.
They are interwoven and interweaving
with all of life,
as Life.

You are like a tree,
a unique tree,
and the seed of your creation
came from the Fruit of Love.

A tree does not desire nor need to compete,
nor does it worry or envy other trees and their fruit.
A tree only needs be integral with its unique nature
and Joy will bloom from its entire being.

Be alive like a tree with a passion to support Life.
Bless the fruits of your loving abundantly
and share with all beings.
A tree doesn't restrict its fruit
only to one or another.
Its wide-opened branch-wings welcome all
into the safe haven of its heart-field.
Its flowers carry the fragrance of Love
for bees and hummingbirds
to make pilgrimage to.
Its roots lie within the heart of the Mother.
Its trunk stands tall with the strength of the Father.
Its leaves dance and play in the wind
like the joy of the Children.

Its fruit contains the seeds of promise
like the potential of the Next Generations.
The seed that made it contains the wisdom
from all its Past Generations.
Its existence honors all,
future, present, past,
for it lives with all,
and all is within it.

By The Grace Of Love!

The rubab of my heart is singing:
Call for everyone!
Come now!
Joy is here!
Joy is here!
My being sings these songs
As I'm being strummed by the grace of Love!

By the grace of Love!
We formed into unique selves,
like flowers blooming from the Tree of Life.

By the grace of Love!
We have made the land bloom with merriness
with the smiling gratitude for Who beats in our hearts.

By the grace of Love!
In the middle of the desert,
without a compass,
my heart is pulled in the direction
of this Ever-Expanding Wondrous Oasis,
the road to Home,
into the Hearts of hearts.

By the grace of Love!
This canvas has been painted with Love's sweetness
so admirers can be whisked into drunken blissfulness,
the fragrance that marries lovers to Beloved.

By the grace of Love!
All sufferings have become blessings.
All happenings become realized for their purpose with the tender gaze of the soul.
What memories once stirred rage and grief now emanate with gratitude and faith.
Every memory has become a reminder,
waking us up to the preciousness
of the Treasure that we have come from,
more valuable than a mountain of gold and precious stones.

By the grace of Love!
Every step I take is in sync with Life's Musical Melody.
Every breath I take is in sync with Earth's Cycle of Generosity.
Everyone I meet is a friend sent from Beyond.
Everything I do is guided from the Eternal Love that exists Within.
Everywhere I look there is a monsoon of blessings pouring.

By the grace of Love!
Come, join, and celebrate,
dance, clap, cheer, and reverberate,
for Love is here
and we are Love!

Beyond Sense And Nonsense

Beyond sense and nonsense…
Beyond thoughts and ideas…
Beyond interpretation and conversation…
Beyond time and space…
There is a Sea of Silence
that screams of our origin:
Love.
Let yourself be washed by This
like the Ocean washes the shoreline
of all things and markings
that are not sand in it's pure form.
Beyond thinking and doing,
I am being…
from Here.

From Here
all is an ever-unfolding,
ever-expanding,
Ever-Ever Land of Miracles.
Sink,
Float,
Swim,
Pour,
For all that you do,
Make sure it comes from Here.
Once you return Here,
you'll remember what lies beyond the veil
of "you" and "me".
Boundless Love.

Enough With The Parrot Talk!

Enough with this talk of
what he said or what she said!
Enough with this regurgitation
of indoctrination!
Enough with this imitation,
attempting to be anyone other than you!
There are too many satisfied
with being the echoes of a parrot,
rambling with replication and repetition.
This is not who you are.
This is not your purpose.

Oh souls of Soul!
Do you know what you are?
Do you know where you're from?
You are a precious gem
from the Beloved's Love-Mine.
You are a Garden of Love
made into a one-of-a-kind rose.
You are Infinity manifesting as moments.
You are the inter-dimensional song of Euphoria.
You are the expansive silence of All-Possibilities.
You are Creation's creation creating
on the edge of a waterfall of flowing novelty.
You originate from your heart,
where life begins,
the portal to the Origin of Love.
Bring your origin-ality to life!

The Lover Of Love

Oh Love!
Everywhere I turn,
Your Fragrance beckons me.
Just one whiff has left me allured,
entranced,
enraptured,
enlivened,
invigorated,
whirling in a tornado storm of passionate frenzy
for the gratitude to be ecstatically alive.

Oh Love!
Where have you taken me?
I am floating beyond all worlds.
A million half-joys cannot compare
to one full timeless moment
of this intoxicating bliss.

Oh Love!
Your Presence has freed my wings of joy from the binds of thought,
like a dove escaping from a cage,
excitedly flying out to freedom.
Your Generosity has opened me
to witness a thousand new dimensions
of this Ocean of Gifting,
that guides all streams and rivers Home.

Oh Love!
You've awakened my heart
with compassionate cries.
These tear-droplets
have washed me anew
the way the morning dew
awakens the garden flower.
I am Your devoted prayer candle
to all those who are yearning.
My flame is Your Loving.

Oh Love!
I've been set aflame in mesmerizing burning.
All I touch is ignited into fervent vividness.
To See You is majestic.
To Know You is ecstasy.
I'm a wild horse racing everywhere to share Your Wine.
Every gallop vigorously screams of Your Essence.

Oh Love!
You've blessed my mind-blindness
and given me soul-sight.
You've lifted all veils with One Glance.
What was once hidden sweetness
can now be vividly seen
as I focus on the happenings between spaces and things,
like the smile the sunflower radiates
to the honeybee it greets.
"As-salaam-alaikum," says the sunflower.
"Wa-alaikum-salaam," says the honeybee.
Gifts are exchanged between the two
and the honeybee departs leaving a loving-trail
that the sunflower looks upon with gratitude.

Like this,
You call beings together
and orchestrate magnificence
through spirited purpose.

For this,
I am a lover of Love.

I've Searched For You

I've searched for You
at the highest peaks,
in the deepest caverns,
through the vibrant rainforests,
by the pristine lakes,
throughout the seven seas
and the seven continents,
at the ancient sites,
at the timeless wonders,
and yet,
I've found You at every-here
and every-there,
at every-where
from no-where,
now-here.

Like a drop of water in the ocean,
I feel Your Pulse at the center of my being
and feel myself beating within Your Heart.
My life is one love poem to another,
You are every inspiration.

Everything You Give

Everything You see
is beautified beyond tenfold.

Everything You bless
blesses generations,
future, current, and past.

Everything You kiss
is electrified with cosmic passion.

Everything You whisper
is richly coated with a sweetness so sweet,
all the world's honeybees would go insane for just a drop.

Everything You touch
melts into rivers of enraptured bliss.

Everything You give
gives on and on,
endlessly,
abundantly,
from one to another,
the way a mulberry tree bears mulberries,
and mulberries bear seeds,
and the seeds bear new mulberry trees,
which grow a green velvety coat of leaves,
which provides sustenance for silkworms to feast upon,
which they transform into silk,

which is sewn into adorned tapestries,
all for the sake of Love.

Oh Spirit of Love!
You've planted the seed of Love at the core of my existence.
Now I've become a gardener of the Heart,
alive to sow Love's seeds in the hearts of all,
all for the sake of You.

In Your Dreaming

In Your Dreaming,
we are dreams manifesting.

In Your Calling,
we are adventures embarking.

In Your Guiding,
we are joy sailing.

In Your Blessing,
we are destinies creating.

In Your Seeing,
we are awe-filled wandering.

In Your Speaking,
we are stories unfolding.

In Your Hearing,
we are songs of yearning.

In Your Loving,
we are passion unbridling.

In Your Knowing,
we are humility bowing.

In Your Giving,
we are Love aborning.

In Your Receiving,
we are Paradise living.

In Your Heart
we live,
we dance,
we sing,
we drink,
we are.

Oh Great Heart!

Oh Great Heart!
You've opened me beyond myself.
You've placed me exactly where I must be
to meet who I must meet,
give what I must give,
receive what I must receive,
feel what I must feel,
experience what I must experience,
all of it guided by Love.
Seconds have stretched into Infinity
and Majesty has filled the space.
I tick-tock between this vast spaciousness
to Love's Rhythmic Music.
Light-wings expand.
Where I once thought I was falling,
Your Loving has lifted me in flight
and taken me through all dimensions
so as to realize that reality is always more than it seems.

Oh Great Heart!
Your Love has filled me
with Knowing
to my age-old questions:
What is my purpose?
Why am I here?
To remind these human beings
that we are all a flock of angels
by the way I exist

and the way I greet them.
To bring more souls
into the depths
of Your Love-Ocean.
To bring this Heaven
to every-where.
To bless the way
You have blessed me
into this enrapturing existence.

Oh Great Heart!
I can no longer speak
with only tongue.
My whole being hums
to the Beat of Your Love.

Oh Great Guardian Of Love!

Oh Great Guardian of Love!
You pierce the illusory fog
with Your Brilliance.
Some say this Light is blinding.
It is only the mind that is blinded
with radiance it can never comprehend.
While those eyes are closed,
another set opens,
the intuitive eyes.
Now they can see
this Field of Consciousness.
"This is the way Home",
the soul says.
Like dust motes dancing around a ray of light,
You enliven and uplift souls with Purpose
as they make flight-circles of Joy.

Where Are You From?

An innkeeper asks a lover,
"Where are you from?"

The lover answers,
"From the Heart of hearts.
From the Love of lovers.
From the Soul of souls.
From the Joy of joys."

The innkeeper stares with confusion.
"I'm from this town.
Where are you from?"

The lover rejoices at the opportunity
to remind a soul of where home is.
The lover grabs a fistful of sand,
then looks over to the innkeeper and says,
"Like the sand passing through my hand,
I am a visitor of this world,
just as you are,
just as every-thing is.
Where we come from?
Love's Eternal Music."

Lovers know that they belong to Love,
that they are made of Love,
that they are Love,
and yet,

their hearts strum ecstatically
for more of this Wine.
Passion never runs dry
for these drunkards of Divinity.
In their drinking,
they become the glass,
the wine,
and the Tavern.
Sacred Diversity.
Euphoric Oneness.
This is the lover's homeland.

Teach Me How To Live

Oh God!
Teach me the secret
to living wonderfully.

Dear soul,
Look upon all you see
with the eyes of pure wonder.
See majestic worlds shining
within everyone's eyes.
This is how one lives
a wonderful life.

Oh God!
Teach me the secret
to living joyfully.

Dear soul,
Let the joy of the Beloved's Heart
from which you live within
outpour and fill
this sacred space between all life
like the Sun's warmth enlivening
a field of wildflowers into cheerful blooming.
This is how one lives
a joyful life.

Oh God!
Teach me the secret
to living passionately.

Dear soul,
Know that all you see
came from a spark of Infinity.
Become the expression of this Cosmic Passion
which made the galaxies and stars
and all beings whirl in this ever-expanding
celebration of Life.
Share Creation's exhilarating joy
by your full enthusiastic beingness.
This is how one lives
a passionate life.

Oh God!
Teach me the secret
to living purposefully.

Dear soul,
Let your every step,
your every breath,
your every decision
be guided by the emerging
serendipities and synchronicities.
Be Love's Prayer and Love's Answering
to all that you meet on your path.
This is how one lives
a purposeful life.

The Loudest Sound

There is a sound louder than all others,
that makes galaxies form
and worlds spin in a perfect harmonic dance.
Its echoes first struck at the dawn of creation
and have reverberated throughout the infinite future.
Everything we say is overpowered
by the profound volume of this sound:
Silence.

In the center of this silence,
I hear a hundred universes unraveling.
I see countless rose gardens opening to the Mighty Sun.
An outpouring of wondrous nectar emerges.
Sweet truth flows from this honeycomb of silence.
All truth is told by this silence.
You know this when you look upon another.
Their silent essence speaks more in a moment
than what's contained in a volume of information.
All language is merely an interpretation.
Don't forget the origin of what's being said.
It comes from neither you nor I,
but from this silent realm of pure consciousness.
Let Silence speak through you
and the words and non-words will materialize
with graceful knowing of what must be expressed.

Love's Prayer Rug

Oh Love!
With just one sip of Your Wine,
I am rendered in humility,
praying for more.
I've lost all need
for reason and understanding
in Your Intoxicating Glory.
How foolish I was
to seek understanding
of something so beyond
all comprehension.
I'm but a grain of salt
in Your Ocean.
I faithfully float in Your Knowingness.
Carry me with Your Love-Waves.
Let me explore all of Your Lovingness.

Dear soul!
If you wish to explore
the Majesty of Love,
pray in the heart-temples
of all those around you.
Everywhere you stand
is Love's Prayer Rug.

Humanity's Prayer And Answering

There is a sacred merging
with energy-breath-sound-movement-awareness.
I place my hands on my body
and the body's primordial rhythms overtake me.
E-motion permeates the space within and around.
I cannot even focus mind.
Spirit is the one listening.
What am I?
A culmination of all of this?
A Knowing answers.
I am a being of consciousness,
unraveling,
reorganizing,
as Life's Wisdoms reshape me
as an embodiment of Love
aligned with the promise for my incarnation.
We were conceived as humanity's prayer.
We were born to be part of the answering.
How we live our lives is how we fulfill
the promise that birthed us.

As I Pray

As I pray,
I become the prayer.
As I bless,
I become the blessing.
As I thank,
I become the gratitude.
As I love,
I become the pulse
of the Beloved's Heart.
As I become silent,
I become the boundless boom
of Creation's Echo.
This silence is filled
with soundless sounds
at infinite volumes
that restore my being
as Rapture's Ringing.
In this majestic placeless place,
possibilities blossom and bloom
like ever-unfolding roses
from the Garden of Eternity.
Just one whiff of a single rose here
will leave you chanting Love
with the expression of your being
for the rest of existence and non-existence.

Dear soul,
Stop all endless searching,
slip into this silence,
and let your smelling be filled
with the fragrance of these roses.

Seen, Unseen, Heard, Unheard

Oh God!
What am I to do?
I feel invisible amongst everyone!
Unseen.
Unheard.
In so much pain.

Dear soul,
Are you invisible to yourself?
Do you recognize the Light that's made you,
that shines through your authentic expression,
the Light you are?
If you cannot see it for yourself,
seek it within all life around you.
Know this secret and practice it frequently.
Whatever you feel is lacking
in your life,
in yourself,
bring forth that essence
for others.
You say you feel invisible and unheard.
What a gift!
You know how it feels for all the others now!

Why do you know?
Why is this a gift?

Because in your design,
you were carefully crafted
to be one who sees the unseen
and hears the unheard.
Bring presence to this Brilliance
that's at the core of every being.
Praise it!
Make others feel seen and heard.
Know that in your praising
of this Light within others
you praise the very existence
of this Light within yourself!
Souls are luminous and brightly visible.
Come out from your hiding
behind the curtains of your-self.

Enough?

Enough?
Enough with this non-sensical chatter
about not being enough.
Don't fall for the mind's trickery.
Those thoughts aren't yours.
Thoughts are as solid as clouds,
they disintegrate in the presence of the Sun.
Let the Light of Truth shine
and watch these thought-clouds
fade away into Love.

Enough?
Why downgrade from your true nature?
Think of what you're made from!
You are made from the Infinite,
have you forgotten that?
Is the Infinite just "enough"?
Is Creation just "enough"?
Staring at illusions will leave one deluded.
With your incarnation being shorter than a blink in eternity,
you don't have time to waste
on such foolish matters.

You are the love of Love,
the desire of the Designer,
the dream of the Dreamer,
the kiss of the Beloved
blown into existence.

Within the pupil of your eyes
are hidden galaxies.
Go on and bless all
with this fragrance of Love
you call your soul.

The Lover's Entire Being

The lover's entire being pulsates with intoxicating desire
like a flamenco guitar
strumming in an ever-growing passionate frenzy.
Entranced in Love's euphoria,
every word that escapes the lover's mouth,
every breath that escapes the lover's nostrils,
every note that escapes the lover's instrument,
mutters out with fervent longing
for more of the Beloved.

The lover swims in the Love-Fermented Wine-Ocean,
the Heart of the Beloved,
and yet ardently yearns for more drink.
No amount will quench their ever-expanding thirst
for more of this Nectar.

The tavern door is open.
All are blessed with this ageless wine.
Crowds of cheerful souls enter.
The tavern owner says,
"There is more than enough for everyone!"
There is no running out from where
this tavern owner sources this Wine.

Surrender To Joy

With fiery tenacity,
this determined mind
sets to climb mighty mountains.
They reach the top
and are quick to search
for the next mountaintop.
Summit after summit,
they grow wearier and wearier.
Finally, weariness stops them in their tracks.
They think, "Failure!"
"Surrender," says their inner-knowing.
They fall to the ground,
on their backs,
arms wide opened,
floating on the clouds of liberation.
They erupt with ecstatic laughter.
Joy is reborn.

Behind the incessant hunger
of endlessly searching to prove oneself
is the neglected childlike playfulness
that looks at life with awe-filled wonder
and finds miracles in raindrops.
Surrender to this adventurous spirit
that liberates the passionate expression
of your true nature.
Let it guide you like the Ocean guides waves.
There is no growing up
without growing joy.

Inhale...Exhale...

This Grand Majesty
has blessed our senses
to observe the Beloved
in every part of this interconnected web of life!
Watch the marvel unravel
in front of yourself!
The trees inhaling
humanity's exhaling.
Humanity inhaling
the trees' exhaling.
This cycle of giving
is designed into the very core
of all of us.

You came a spark of Love
from the union of mother and father.
When you leave,
what lives on is your legacy of deeds,
how you loved and blessed.
The apple is eaten
and left for decomposition.
It takes on new form
as the seeds within it
form new trees.
Its other counterparts
become fertile ground
and energy for living life.
However, even insects won't eat
that which had no love inside.

Look at this tender joy you feel
after you help the helpless.
Look at this enrapturing love you feel
after you bless another.

The Addiction Of Truth

Truth leaves an addictive imprint
on the mind of every seeker.
Once they've tasted the Truth,
they always want more.
They passionately seek it
in every conversation,
in every encounter,
in every moment.
They ask,
"What is True here?"
Like the Sun piercing the fog,
Truth answers.

Hurricane Of Love

You exhale
a hurricane of Love,
sweeping away all illusions,
leaving only Truth.

I'm free of myself,
intoxicated,
by Love's Enrapturing Fragrance.
All time and space fade
and I am One
with the Weaver of Creation.

They say,
"Home is where the heart is."
I say,
"Home is in Your Heart.
That is where to find me."

In the silent hours,
I hear so much conversation
between Your Heart and my heart.
Only Truth.
Only Love.
Only Gratitude.
Only Light.
Only the Music that organizes creation's ecstatic pulsations.
My heart is only a portal to You.
Can I even call anything "mine"?

There Is A Sweetness Beyond Sweetness

There is a Sweetness
sweeter than the sweetest baklava.
There is a Brightness
brighter than the brightest star.
There is a Stillness
stiller than the stillest mountain.
There is a Lightness
lighter than the lightest feather.
There is a Clearness
clearer than the clearest mirror.
There is a Quietness
quieter than the quietest cave.
There is a Deepness
deeper than the deepest depths.
There is a Warmness
warmer than the warmest hearth.
There is an Emptiness
emptier than the emptiest air.
There is a Sharpness
sharper than the sharpest blades.
There is a Tenderness
more tender than the most tender caress.
There is a Drunkenness
drunker than that of the drunkest drunkard.
There is a Spaciousness
more spacious than the cosmic skies.
There is a Liveliness
livelier than the liveliest festivals.

There is a Wakefulness
more wakeful than the dawn's rising.
There is an Adventurousness
more adventurous than journeying the planet.
There is a Wondrousness
more wondrous than the wonder of the night sky.
There is a Beautifulness
more beautiful than the most beautiful of faces.
There is a Blissfulness
more blissful than the summer breeze.
There is a Pureness
purer than the purest water.

Drink from this.
Breathe from this.
Live from this.
Be from this.
Dance from this.
Sing from this.
Paint from this.
Speak from this.
Find all of this
within your heart.
Lose yourself
within This Heart
and become more than "you" ever could.

What Good Is A Heart Without Love?

What good is language
without meaning?
What good is art
without color?
What good is home
without warmth?
What good is travel
without adventure?
What good is work
without purpose?
What good is sleep
without dreams?
What good is sound
without silence?
What good is prayer
without God?
What good is freedom
without surrender?
What good is lover
without Beloved?
What good are wings
if you won't fly?
What good is the rose
without fragrance?
What good is the songbird
without song?
What good is the egg
without new life?

What good is the nest
without nurturing?
What good is the candle
without flame?
What good is the night sky
without stars?
What good is a day
without wonder?
What good is a mirror
without reflection?
What good is pollen
without bees?
What good is honeycomb
without honey?
What good is honey
without sweetness?
What good are we
without each other?
What good is the fish
without the ocean?
What good is a heart
without Love?

The Myth Of Sensitivity

There is a great myth
that sensitivity is weakness.
Anyone who lives life wide-awake
will sense more of the spectrum of life.
Sensitivity is a super power.
It helps us feel beyond the veil,
beyond ourselves,
beyond the mask of thought,
to discover what truly lies
beyond, beneath, between realities.
Those who've been cracked open
have been blessed to wake up
from the numbing comfort.
Numbness is weakness.
You weren't made of dullness.
We are born from the Phenomenal.
Come out of this spell
by expressing your true nature.

Only the sensitive
can sense the whispers of the Heart.
These courageous ones
are the ones that live
a majestic adventure
with every heartbeat.
Any evolutionary pioneer
felt more than what's common.
Transcend commonality.

Compassion is your compass.
You are meant to bless more;
otherwise, you wouldn't sense
their silent cries.

The Kiss That Blows Existence

Oh God!
I'm in awe
with how you connect us!
I'm in surrender
with how you inter-direct us!
I'm in joy
with how you orchestrate us!

I am a kiss
blown into existence
from Your Eternal Love.
Ever since I've left
the Lips of my Beloved,
I've longed to go back.

I recognize Your Presence
in the space between
they and me.
Your Love is magnetic
magnetizing souls together.

Oh God!
I would give my self…
I would give my life…
to live in this space
from which You Conduct from!

I used to pray out to You
hoping for an answer
until I realized Your Brilliance
in the weaving of all of us together.
The portal to You exists
at the center of our beings:
our hearts.

You've interwoven us
with Your Love
to make us both
prayer and answer
to one another.

Now,
I pray in the hearts of others
because that's the direction
where I find You.

I am lost,
adrift,
so far from shore,
unsure which direction
will take me home.
I'm so thirsty.
I taste the water.
It's Wine.
I jump overboard
and drink myself full.
I put a message in a bottle.
It reads: myself.
Send this message elsewhere.
I live in Your Love-Ocean Depths.
I am one with Your Love-Currents.

Everywhere I turn,
anyone I see,
is another one of Your Kisses
blown into existence.

The Special Friendship

There is a special friendship
that goes beyond words and stories,
beyond joking and laughing,
beyond hellos and goodbyes,
one that is a sacred mirror
reflecting the divinity
within two lovers
to one another.

When two souls sit in that space
gazing into the depths of
each other's being,
a third essence emerges of the two
and two becomes One.
Angels sing choirs at the sight
of these kinds of unions.

It's these friendships where
one look into another's soul
opens up a hundred universes,
where first-time encounters
ignite a soul familiarity,
a remembrance,
a sense that this meeting
has been scheduled On Purpose for you both.
It has.

Your instructions lie in their heart,
and theirs lie in your heart.
Stargaze into the cosmic depths
of one another
and uncover the sacred mysteries
that are begging to be discovered.

The Mystic, The Cup, The Wine

In between this celebration
of sights and sounds
and colors and senses
live those who crave the Origin,
the Source,
the Scent beyond scents
and the Texture beyond textures…
these mystics.

Their hearts are barrels
with an endless supply of wine.
Their wine is fermented
in their ever-deepening yearning for God.
They find novelty and Majesty
in everywhere and everyone.
They're reasonless drunks,
willing to go to any lengths
for more of this Pure Wine.

There's no small talk with them!
They seek the essence
of the essence
within the essence of conversation.
Every conversation pours
soul-drunkenness.
Your being gets stained
with this Wine of Love.
People pass by you

and can't help but to wonder,
"What is it about them?"

Joy spreads its grin
ear to ear
as the lover is transported
throughout the Seven Heavens
and the Earth.
Ascended,
whirling in beingness,
at-one-ment with Beloved,
this cosmic rapture
is purpose for the mystic.
This is why you see them
always filling their cups with others.
"Drink up!
Drink until you, cup, and wine
cease to exist as separate!"

Love's Rain

Sink into the depths
of Beloved's Heart
and become the pulse
of kindness
to everyone,
to everywhere.
Emerge Love-born and purified.
Be the prayer's answer.

Life is too short
for you not to live as a blessing.
The blesser's blessing blesses
an enveloping field of Love
between blesser, blessed,
and all in between and around.
Bless with conscious beingness.

What happens when a fallen angel
rises back to Love?
What happens when the seed
from an apple that fell from the tree
is nourished with raining blessings?
It rises as a host for life
and unfolds as miraculous purpose.
Rain is radical with kindness and generosity.
It doesn't say, "You can be blessed
and you will not."
It sprays its love-shower for all.
Be Love's Rain.
Shower kindness everywhere.

How You Answer The Call

There's an adventure
calling to your heart,
begging you to start
that journey for which
you've been made for.

It speaks to you in dreams.
It knocks at the door
of your consciousness.
It steers your focus
onto everyday messages
to recognize the signs
hidden in Life's passages.
Serendipities,
synchronicities,
all Love's workings,
all Love's guidance.
All happening
to bring you Home.
Are you aware?

Many ignore this calling of Soul.
They'd rather be caught up
in their own idea or someone else's
of what life should be.
Then things don't work
the way they "should be"
and their life falls apart.

So one begins soul-searching
for what's been present from the start.

All the wise suggest
that you never leave to rest
the calling of the soul,
how you answer is your test.
Answer with the passion
that created this world.
Answer with the hunger
that lovers have for Beloved.
Answer with the answer
that Life made into you.

Diversity

Celebrate the vast range
of perspectives.
Nothing is limited to
a single dimension,
or even a few,
or even many.
In this holographic universe,
we see what we are
in everything…
in everyone.

If what you seek is growth,
surround yourself with differences
that stretch your mind,
that ignite your soul.
All journeys take someone
from one place through many others,
the place they observed the world from
into a fuller, expanded perspective.

Life thrives richly
in the rainforest.
You see such variety,
from tree frog to croc,
from panther to songbird,
from viper to pitcher plant.
Rich diversity floods the environment
with the revelrous gathering

of uniqueness and Oneness,
the joy of being alive in Life.

Go to the desert,
where life seems more barren,
and observe each grain of sand.
Each makes up the desert
and yet each appears different.

Go to your garden
and notice that even the roses
wear different shades of lipstick.
They smile as the honeybee lands
taking pollen and leaving the rose
with a taste of its travels.
Each blade of grass is unique
and part of the entire Earth.

Go to the tundra
and hear arctic wolves
howl through the night sky.
Each howl has a distinctive pitch
and in unison they blend
in one cry of longing.

Gaze upon the moonless night sky.
Enamor in the illustrious presence
of the stars and solar systems
echoing their unique light-presences
from millions-to-billions of years ago
to present-moment sight.
Let your eyes fill
with the awe of
hundreds of billions of stars,
all part of the cosmos.

See the Universe within each star
and feel the Passion
that created such vibrant splendor.
This is what flows
through your veins.

Go into the ocean
and find a new world
swimming with life.
Life is a spectrum.
Each color is made of Love.
Love takes you beyond sight,
beyond senses,
beyond here-and-now,
behind the curtain of time-space,
to Infinite Warmth and Infinite Light,
where you spin around with all else
like leaves dancing to the Rhythm of Wind
within this home where the Heart is.

This Fragrance

What is this fragrance
that with one inhale
I breathe in a new world?

It is a fragrance so potent,
ten-thousand roses fall outwards
in their blossoming open
when its presence is in the air.

Its allure brings swans into dance.
Both bowing to one another,
"Namaste," says one.
"Namaste," says the other.
They circle one another
until two circles merge
into one Love-Current.
Praise be to this union,
for it is this fragrance
that guides beings into this Union
where you-and-I-become-One.

The heart weeps
at the sight of such beauty.
Its sole desire is Union
with the Heart to which it belongs.
It yells to Love,
"Take me prisoner!
Throw the keys away!

Never let me out
from the chambers of Your Heart!
Have me sweep the floors,
anything.
My existence
is my gift for You.
My existence
is my prayer to You."
Such devotion fills
every corner of every room
with Love's Euphoric Passion.

Lovers fall to their knees,
humbled and devoted.
They kiss the Earth
everywhere they go.
"God bless God," they say
through the essence of their essence.

We are living prayers
through the intentionality of our focus.
Recognize all unions
like the swans do.
Only blessing.
Only praise.

Finding Treasure

Oh human being
who searches everywhere
for some meaning to your existence,
you've searched all the places,
sought any traces,
and yet your map has not
lead you to the Treasure.
You've searched everywhere
but the center of your being
and the source of others' beingness.
You've sought everywhere
and forgotten what lays in plain sight,
right before your eyes,
this no-thing-ness
from which every-thing be-comes.

Where do you think
you think from?
Where do you believe
you believe from?
Where do you know
you know from?
Go back to where "you" came from.
Find yourself in this infinite field.

There is a timeless presence
that magnifies anything
under its lens.

You've been given a gift:
a magnifying glass.
Be conscious of what you put it over.

Move and be moved by the sacred dance
between desire, desired, and desirer.
At the core of the soul's desire
is the scent of sweetness
bringing you home.
This is where the treasure lies.

Ever Since I Was Created

Ever since I was created,
my nose has been transfixed
on the scent
of Love's abundant feast.
My soul waters
for these euphoric flavors
of this ecstatic atonement.
I am desire
longing for this Source.

I searched around the world
and knocked on many doors,
seeking Beloved.
I'd yell with full beingness,
"Where is the One I Love?"
A door finally opens
and a joy comes running out,
eager to embrace me
and welcome me Home.
Love answers those who knock from within.

Heartbreak Or Heartwake?

Dear Soul,
This heartbreak you feel
is not the end,
it is your beginning.
It is your freedom.
A plant may look nice
in a vase,
but it thrives
in the fertile grounds
of this soil-like mess.
Every being undergoes a hatching.
The bird,
the frog,
the butterfly,
the human,
all originate from an egg.
This is not heartbreak,
this is your heart-wake.
This is your hatching
from yourself
into Love.

Love's Fermentation

Why do You fill my eyes
with the tears of humanity?
Why do You fill my heart
with the heartbreak of creation?
You are Benevolence!
Why treat me with such burdens?
Why take me from my course of life
and throw me into the alleys of pain
and the corridors of suffering?
Why drag me by the feet
to everywhere I've longed to avoid?
I plead for Mercy!

Love answers
and what I thought was a curse
becomes realized blessing.
I turn to what was once my agony
and my heart screams with ecstasy,
"Oh Love!
You've given me oceans of compassion!
You've given me depth into human be-ing!
You've crushed me like grapes,
fermented sadness,
and made me into wise wine!
You've granted me the honor
to walk out of my heart
as a medicine,
to bless every aching heart

by observing through Your Beloved Eyes.
What I thought was my shipwreck
was my arrival into Your Heart.
Give me more!
Ferment me in You!
Let me become
aged wine in Your Loving!
For Love's Sake,
I exist!"

You Are The Promise Fulfilling

We are travelers,
foreigners,
visitors,
from the realm of Eternal Love,
manifested as soul-being,
experiencing the vast spectrum
of Cosmic Expression.

Fret not
about what's to come
in the future
or what brings pain
from the past.
Fill your worries
with the wine of your essence.
In your transfixed drunkenness
you'll realize what you are.

You are Infinity
born as a moment.
You are Desire
manifesting.
You are the Divine Memory
and the Sacred Future Vision.
You are the Promise
fulfilling.

Being Purpose

Oh prisoner of time,
free yourself from your own bonds.

Come out of yourself
and return to Omni-Love.

Marvel at the Marvelousness
that orchestrates this Symphony
that births forests from a single seed.

Earth crashes into itself
and mountain ranges are born,
hosting an ecosystem of life.

Unfold yourself from yourself
like the rose,
blooming outwards
and blessing all
with the sweet fragrance of Home.

Doves flap their elegant wings in prayer
enthusiastically praising freedom.

The sun paints illustrious designs,
making pastel clouds glimmer Heaven's colors
simply by shining its radiant beauty.

You search through libraries,
read the stars,
consult teacher after teacher,
to find your purpose.

Being is the purpose
you've been seeking all along.

No Sleep For The Soul

How is it that
I close my eyes
and wake up elsewhere,
living,
observing,
experiencing,
dreaming,
feeling,
hearing,
seeing…
and then I open my eyes
and wake up again
into another elsewhere?

And then here,
in this world called reality,
I blink for a moment
and disappear into nothingness
only to open my eyes
and see a new world emerge.

Which is the dream?
Which is reality?
Are both dreams
and both reality?
Where is it
that I truly live?
Where is it

that I'm just visiting?
Where did I fall asleep?

I close my eyes again
and a familiar rhythm
takes me between
existence and non-existence.
I disperse in realization.
There is no such thing
as sleep for the soul.
Only more wakefulness.
Only more passion.
Only more wonderment.
Only more love.

The Placeless Place

When you're out of ideas,
feel like there's no creative spark,
can't add color to the blank canvas,
open your arms
in wide embrace
and fall back into
the placeless place
of timeless time
where everything
becomes one ocean of no-thing.

Fall so deep
that you lose your-self,
dematerializing
in the infinite void
of infinite spaciousness.

From Eternal No-thing-ness
came the cosmic spark.
From Eternal No-thing-ness
sparks flew everywhere
and these fires became galaxies
filled with stars,
filled with Magic.

Dear soul,
you are a spark of Eternity.
You transcend ideas.

You are Creation's creativity.
Your life is a tapestry within the Tapestry.
What you seek is what you are.
You need not paint,
only polish,
and creativity,
ideas,
brilliance,
marvel
will shine everywhere you are.
You are Love's mirror
reflecting Love
to Love.

Breathe Like A Lover

Here is a simple secret
available to all.
Wherever you feel less,
wherever aches,
wherever pains,
wherever needs energy,
needs love,
needs life…
breathe from where you have,
experience,
are more,
abundance,
love,
healing,
energy,
alive.

Breathe from the more
and let that breath flow
like the summer breeze
carrying love stories
over to where there's less.

Breathe from the abundance
and let the Ocean fill
where there is lack.

Breathe from the love
and let it flood the worthlessness
with Majesty,
like the mountain spring
filling pools of shimmering beauty.

Breathe from the energy
that created the galaxies,
the sun,
the stars,
and let it engulf,
energize,
where there was no spark.

Breathe from the aliveness,
the special magic
that makes dead stems
sprout new rose buds.

Apply this principle
anywhere and everywhere,
always focusing more on the more,
and bringing more where there is less,
and you'll witness reality unfold
from what seemed like endless stagnation.

Lovers breathe out
multiple the love they breathe in.
They long to share this passion,
this mystic mist.
Breathe like a lover
and exhale a new vision into reality.

Pour Yourself Through Myself

Oh,
this gap,
between what I am
and what I must become…

Oh,
this pain,
of knowing reality
and living with this illusory matrix…

Oh,
this sorrow,
of hearing the cries
of humanity
and feeling so helpless
to answer…

Oh,
this misery,
of focusing on my life
instead of playing my part with life…

Oh,
this distress,
between what I'm doing
and what I must do…

Oh,
this agony,
of sleepwalking
when I am to be daydreaming…

Oh,
this suffering,
between living as separate me
and living as a collective we…

Oh,
this depression,
of feeling so alone
and knowing we are all-one…

Oh,
this anguish,
of trying so hard
when I know to surrender…

Oh,
this sadness,
from knowing potential
and not living it…

Oh,
this tragedy,
of feeling so helpless
when I am meant to help the helpless…

Oh,
this madness,
of seeing two separate worlds
when I live between them…

Oh,
this foolishness,
of tasting rapture
and living flavorless…

Oh,
this heartache,
of yearning for You
while living in You…

Oh,
this affliction,
that torments my soul
in its desire to dissolve into You…

Oh,
this hardship,
of living in this realm
and knowing I'm from elsewhere…

Oh,
this torture,
of knowing Your Scent
and endlessly searching for You…

Oh,
Dear Beloved,
You have blessed me
with me what I thought
was a curse.
What was once darkness
fills with the purpose
to be a lantern
for souls everywhere.
Pour Yourself

through myself.
Let swirling galaxies
fill this gap
and manifest miracles
where there was once hopelessness.

Who? What? Why?

Who am I?
Why am I here?
What am I?
Who made me?

These questions watchfully haunt me
like the moonlight
staring upon life.
There are no hidden alleyways;
there is no place to hide.
When I am silent,
the orchestra of curiosity is at play.
But when I fall into that deep place
where I no longer exist,
I hear Your Voice.

"I am the Artist,
you are the inspiration.
I am the Weaver,
you are what's woven.
I am the Wine,
you are the drunkard.
I am the All-Knowing,
you are the all-curious.
I am the Composer,
you are the muse.
I am the Mirror,
you are the reflection.

I am the Lantern,
you are the moth that dances around it.
I am the Ocean,
you are a wave.
I am the Field,
you are the shepherd.
You are a spark
of the Infinite.
I am the Sun,
you are the particles
that dance in ecstasy.
You are the love of Love.
You are the desire of Desire.
You are the inspiration of Spirit.
You are the glory of the Glorious.
You are the magnificence of the Magnificent.
You are as much a part of Me
as I am of You."

"If that is so,
why did You place
such sorrow in my heart?"

"To remind you
that true joy is found
in being woven
with all the other threads
that make up My Quilt.
Only in the illusion of separateness will you find sorrow.
All hearts are part of the One Heart"

The Gift Of Potential

The gift of potential
is found in its realization.
This process of realization
is the alchemy
that makes the formless into form
and the form into formless.
It is what makes the hardest ice
into flowing streams of fluid water.
It is what makes the fullness of water
into the invisible kiss of vapor.
It is what makes carbon into diamond,
liquid into crystal,
lava into land,
rain into forest,
sperm and egg
into human.
It is what makes dream into reality
and realizes reality as dream.
It is what spins galaxies from nothingness
and what puts galaxies within eyes
for eyes to see galactic wonder everywhere.

To realize
one must use their real eyes,
this observer,
which with its pure observation alone
unmasks new potential
where there were once only walls.

Lovers realize everything
with the eyes of the Beloved,
and thus everything
is an adorned blessing.

Dark Night Of The Soul

I used to wonder
when oh when
would this dark night
finally come to an end…
this seemingly endless
dark night of the soul.

Now I look back and laugh!
Once a lover has tasted
the wine of the soul,
they know that there's
no such thing
as a dark night
where there's soul.

The dark night
is but a veil,
a fabrication
made by the mind.
It's endlessness
serves one purpose…
to allow the mind
to run the show.

It's soul
that makes one thousand veils
fall away
like dead leaves in the wind.

It's soul
that inspires mind
to become a servant of Love.
The night becomes filled
with radiant brilliance
turning darkness
into cosmic wonderland.

Every night with soul
is a night spent
in the Tavern of Love.
Every night with soul,
barrels of gratitude
fill the hearts of lovers
and they become tornados
whirling in ecstasy,
singing rhapsodies
of God
for God.

The Balm

There is a Balm
that gets administered
on the hearts of lovers
who feel the greatest
heartbreak…
The sense of separation
between lover and Beloved.

This Balm
comes to the lover's heart
like a cloud of light
floating down from Heaven,
coated with the eternal sweetness
of Beloved's kiss.

This Balm permeates
the lover's being
with Love's hymn.

The old song of tragedy
gets replaced
with surrendering glory.
A new Heartbeat emerges
and its harmonious rhythm
overtakes lover with Beloved
until all that's left
is One Love.

The lover laughs
in drunken ecstasy.
"How foolish I was
to think You and I
were ever separate.
My heart is
made of Yours…
belongs to Yours…
is Yours.
I dance
in Your depths
tipsily whirling
in Cosmic wonderment
as Love spins me."

Oh God! Where Are You?

Oh God!
Where are You?
Why do You taunt me
with such short visitations
that are eternities in moments?
Why do You ferment my soul into wine
and then leave me for so long that I become vinegar?
Without Your Light,
I am a candle without a flame.
Without Your Guidance,
I am a camel lost in the desert.
Without Your Grace,
I am the most helpless.
Without Your Love,
I am nothing.

I've succumbed to this suffering
like the apple falling from the tree.
My life decomposes.
All I've worked for,
all I've valued,
all that was important to me,
has faded away into nothingness.
Only these apple seeds remain,
seeds that I had forgotten,
the seeds of my soul.
Life weathers me down
into the ground

and I am with it…
all of it.
Then,
a silence emerges
and the birth of an apple tree begins.

Oh God!
How foolish of me to ever doubt You.
How foolish of me to think You ever left me.
The source of everything lives within its creations.

What I thought was my end
was Our Beginning.
I laugh thunderstorms
as I realize
that You were always
within me,
and I within You.

Even The Smallest Spark

Even the smallest
spark of Light
makes monstrous shadows
vanish and hide
in corners.

The flicker of one candle,
of one soul,
illuminates truth
where there was once
an illusory matrix.

Light pierces through
the seemingly endless,
seemingly immersed,
seemingly sealed
ceiling of clouds
and makes way
for the Sun.

With full overhead Sun,
there is no room
for shadow.
Only Light.
Only Truth.
Only Reality.
Only space for lovers
to make use of their wings.

Forget Mindfulness

Forget mindfulness…
Lose your mind
in Love's fermentation.

Become the sweet wine
of soulfulness.

Enter taverns
all across the world
and fill empty cups
with miracles.

You are Love's prayer
and Love's answer.

Eyes Of Infinity

In the midst of chaos,
confusion,
destruction,
demise,
I am pulled out of my body,
out of this physical reality,
to look at this physical reality
through the eyes of limitless reality.

As I observe,
chaos becomes order,
confusion becomes clarity,
destruction becomes renovation,
demise becomes new life.

I thought my life was falling apart,
now I know a new life is falling into place.
Where the caterpillar ends,
the cocoon begins.
When the shell breaks,
beauty arises with glorious wings.

Like this,
when you feel your life crumbling away,
know that you're done crawling…
it's time to use your wings.

A Special Relationship

Rock, Sand, and Wind
share a special relationship.
Rock says to Wind,
"Oh Wind,
rip me apart.
Blend my being
with the Soul of this world.
I am done being Rock,
so stagnant,
so formed.
I miss the formless essence
from which I became.
Shatter me with your alchemy
so I can fly across the world."

Wind weathers down Rock
and makes it Sand.
Wind blows its magical breath
and takes Sand all over the world.
Wind makes Sand into dunes
and beaches
and deserts…
stretching what was
once solid Rock
into flexible mountains,
into new pathways,
into new terrain,
into blissful form.
This Sand-state
is Rock's atonement.

"Thank you, Wind," says Sand,
overjoyed with the spontaneity
each day,
each passing Wind,
brings it.

Wind smiles,
"The pleasure is mine, dear friend.
Although I travel the world,
I have grown lonesome
doing so by myself.
I've longed for a travel companion
that is in love
with the Love
that made this world
and that wishes to experience
how Love manifests
in countless ways.
Although I am formless,
my wish is to create form.
You give me that purpose."

"And you make me more."

Such is the relationship
between two lovers
who seek to experience
the Beloved
in every-thing,
in every-where.

Such is the relationship
when lovers become one
with the Beloved.

Beloved's Alchemy

What is this Alchemy
that with one breath of passion
makes new worlds unravel
from nothingness?

What is this Magic
that opens the floodgates of Love
where it was once dammed?

What is this Mystery
that entices endless hunger,
that keeps my soul on its toes
at the turn of each page,
the passing of each moment,
leaving me wanting more?

What is this Sweetness
that enchants the planets
to dance around the Sun
in wondrous praise?

What is this Balm
that transforms curse into blessing,
pain into medicine,
misery into ecstasy?

What is this Knowing
that makes belief vanish

into timeless faith and awe
for the unraveling of the unknown into known?

I've traversed the world
in search of treasures
and hidden gems,
only to realize
how foolish I'd been.
The gems I've been seeking
are the Wisdoms
that create
creation.

I am entranced,
transfixed,
by the glory of these Wisdoms.
I am euphorically humbled
to realize that such Divinity
created me.

Please,
take this soul you've made me
make my life whatever You wish.
Here is the pen,
here is the paper,
write me how you wish.

Please,
take this life you've given me
and make it a love song
that calls souls
into sweet rejoice
and mesmerized praise,
like the planets that dance
around the Sun.

Who Is This Friend?

Who is it that stands beside me
when I'm seemingly completely alone?
Who is it that embraces me
when I feel so inadequate?
Who is it that guides me
from nowhere to somewhere
and from somewhere to no-where?
Who is it that makes such rich wine
from such great sorrow?
Who is it that makes endless boredom
spin into galaxies of joy?
Who is it that is no "it"
and is part of every "it"?
Who is this Friend
that brings all of us together
for mystical song,
for celestial dance,
for enraptured laughter,
for cosmic celebration,
for Love's appreciation?

All rivers and streams
seek to make their way
back to the Ocean.
The Friend is that Love-current
which guides us
and reminds us
that we've always been part

of the Ocean of Love,
and that the Ocean of Love
courses through our very existence.

Love's riptide pulls us
into this ecstatic realization.
Our stories become One Story
circulating within the
Heart of Beloved.

The Frog And The Pond

A frog leaned over his lily pad
staring down at the pond's silent stillness.
The sunlight's glimmering reflection
met the frog's eyes.
"What is this beauty I see?" asked the frog.

"It is the beauty the manifests
the stars and the galaxies,
the pond and the grass,
the frog and lily pad," a voice answered.

The frog grew tipsy
and elatedly croaked,
"O please!
Let me sink in this beauty
that makes a frog like me
become the enchanted prince!
Mold my life like clay,
do whatever you wish,
as long as I'm bathed in this holiness."

"Dear frog,
this Light,
this Infinite Beauty you wish for
that you see in me
is the glimmering reflection
of what I see in your eyes,"
said the pond.

Tipsiness took over the frog's mind
and it fell off the lily pad
in complete surrender
into Love's endless abyss.
All mirrors live between the experience of
I am
and
I am not.
Between manifest
and nothingness,
there is a Consciousness.
That Present Stillness
is what glimmers
in the pond,
in the frog,
in the sun,
in the stars,
in your eyes,
in mine.
From this silence,
the whole universe dances.
From this silence,
we fall out of the time-space matrix
and into ecstatic eternity.

Sweet Silence

In a world of endless noise,
of endless distraction,
I seek for that sweet silence
that calls the hummingbirds to flowers,
the ocean waves to shore,
the rainwater to the planted seed,
the summer breeze to my cheek.

This sweet silence
sings thousands of melodies
with a chorus of angels
to my heart
and throughout my entire beingness.

The silent music takes over me
and I become one with the Song.
I was never separate from it.
I am the note and the entire Song within it.
I am the audience and the ensemble.
I am the percussions and the strings.
I move to the beat of life
and I am the Rhythm that beats.

To all those who haven't heard this song yet,
I tell them,
"It's the very song that you were born of.
Lose yourself in the glorious sounds
of that sweet silence."

The Vagabond

I am a vagabond,
always traveling,
always exploring,
seeking life's treasures
around the world.

One afternoon as I camped by a lake,
a fish swam up to the surface.
"What brings you here?" it asked me.

"I am a vagabond,
always traveling,
always exploring,
seeking life's treasures
around the world."

"Why do you travel around the world
to seek what's within you?" the fish asked.

"To marvel at the beauty,
the brilliance,
the unique incarnation
that Love has manifested as
is to praise Beloved in infinite ways."

The fish grew very silent,
and then sunk to the depths of the lake,
mesmerized and elated
by the vastness of Love that surrounds it.

Hope And Faith

Hope and faith share a special friendship.
Hope keeps the candle from losing its flame;
Faith reminds the candle that it was lit from the Great Flame.

All hope is lost when the candle is blown out,
but who's breath blew out the flame?

Magic candles have the ability
to regain their flame
even after it gets blown out
time after time again.

We are magic candles.
The Magic that reignites us
is precisely what hope and faith
wish to remind us.

Candles never lose their flame
by lighting other candles up,
because the source of their flame
is Infinite.

Those candles that burn the brightest
will attract more and more candles
that have had their flames blown out.

What are they to do?
Avoid them?
Ignore them?
Get away from them?
Surround themselves with other candles
that burn bright like themselves?

A candle doesn't lose a flicker of its flame
when lighting up dozens,
hundreds,
thousands,
millions of candles that have lost their connection
with the Great Flame.

The flame was never theirs to begin with.
Billions of candles,
One Great Flame,
Expressing its effulgence
in infinite ways.

O Sweet Gratitude!

Gratitude
is the aroma
that brings lover and Beloved
into an enraptured union.

Gratitude
is the kiss
that makes dead flowers rise into new life
with passionate vigor.

Gratitude
is the blessing
that makes copper into gold,
sorrow into fortune.

O sweet Gratitude,
the nectar of Life,
fill every lover's cup
over and over
until they've drunken themselves
out of the realm of existence and non-existence
and into the Tavern of Love.

Dancing Like Incense Smoke

Like the incense smoke,
I dance between the realms of
I am…
And I am not.
The Invisible has made me visible
for a moment of a moment
of a moment of a moment.
But my soul lives between moments,
between all I've known to be real
and all I've learned to be unreal.

My soul…
if I can even call it "mine".
Between you and me,
they and we,
is this Song.
Soul dances to this Song
in a hypnotic trance,
in mesmerized rapture,
like the incense smoke dances
to the Rhythm of the Wind,
surrendering its whole being,
its whole purpose,
to the One Song,
Uni-Verse.

"Play me!"
Says the flute.
"Whatever note it be!
Be it laughter or crying,
be it sadness or gladness!
I am nothing without You!
And I am no-thing with You!"

Through clay and dust
and a powerful Gust,
the Winds of Creation
organize this Celebration,
this Musical Melody
we call
Life.

The paintbrush is most powerful
when the canvas is blank.
From that position,
new worlds can be born.
Between the paint strokes
is Genesis.

What Keeps You Up At Night

Is there something that keeps you up at night?
Something that keeps you from sleeping…
Something that takes over your mind…
Something that whispers to your soul…
Something you know you must do…
Something you must say…to someone…
Something you have become too consumed with daily life to feel…again…
This mysterious some-thing…
What is it?
Where does it come from?
Why do I hear it…feel it…see it…know it?
Because I must.
Because we must.
Because I am guided.
Because we are guided.
Because I am destined.
Because we are destined.
Because the Orchestra of Life requires our music added to the Ensemble of the One-Song,
the Uni-Verse…
As well as the infinite variations of that Song,
the Multi-Verse.
Because the choir of angels beckons us to join in rejoice.
Because your act is part of the Great Act.
Because the Honeycomb has more sweetness with our addition to it.
Because the Night Sky shines brighter when one more star lights up.
"Then what must I do now?"

You've known all along.
Go on…
Towards that some-thing that speaks to your soul…
And a path will illuminate where it was once dark.

A City In Ruins

Ever since You flickered Your Glance towards me,
I have been left in excruciating agony.
Everything I thought my life was about has collapsed,
like a city in ruins.
Wandering through the rubbles of my past life,
I ache like a camel in search of this Purity.
Then a monsoon comes,
purer than the purest of mountain springs.
I have been washed anew,
from the inside.
Like this,
the Infinite fills spiritual hunger.

Oh Beloved,
before You,
I was animated but lifeless,
caught up with hearsay and daily tasks.
With You,
I am the song played through the reed flute.
Your Love is the breath that plays me.

The Womb

From the depths of women,
all of humanity was nurtured into existence.
Stories and songs from mothers reverberate
throughout the core of infant,
preparing them for life on the outside,
and ultimately,
their soul's destiny.

The Womb is sacred and must be respected as so.
Anything you put in Her is made greater.
Give Her sperm and She makes human.
Give Her a vision and She manifests all the necessary encounters,
meetings, relationships, connections, feelings, inspirations, conversations,
and celebrations required to birth this dream into reality.
Pollute Her and She'll give you Hell.
Enrich Her and She'll take you into the depths of Paradise.

The Womb is the vortex from which infinite possibilities
are birthed into reality.
Within every woman is a portal to the Cosmic Womb.
Within that Cosmic Womb,
we are all wombmates,
like stars clustered across the galaxies,
nurtured within the field of Infinite Love.

A Tribute To Mothers

You took life's smallest ingredients and made my soul into human.
You gave me life's best nutrients and made me from embryo to fetus.
You endured life's greatest physical pain and brought me into this world.
You nurtured me with love and care throughout all my stages,
from boy to man.
You lifted my spirits whenever I fell down and lost hope.
You guided my actions to be kind and grateful.
Your entire life since I was conceived became a selfless service to ensure you've done everything in your power to support the purpose of why I was brought into this world, so that I can become the leader, the embodied angel, the blessing the world needs me to be.
How can a son repay a mother who's given him her whole life?
Who's given him life?
It seems impossible to do in this lifetime.
All I can think of,
all I can hope of is that who I am and how I live blesses all others the way you've blessed me throughout all my stages of life.
To be the gift that keeps on giving, who was gifted this life from you.

Lost

I've lost myself in the tipsiness of longing.
Your Gaze has captured my soul's full attention.
I've lost my ideas in the light of Truth.
Your Voice has silenced my mind with eternal wisdom.
I've lost all reason and become disoriented.
Your Fragrance has made me feverish in love.
I've lost all need for speech and thought.
Your Heart has transformed me into a barrel of wine in the tavern of
Love.
I've lost all desires in my desire for You.
Your Radiance is why I'm ravenously passionate.
I've lost the belief that there was ever anything I lost.
Your Kiss has blown away all illusions.

Oh Beloved!
I beg with my life,
allow me to be Your servant.
All is made of Love.
All belongs to Love.
Allow me the gift of your blessed guidance.
I will do whatever Love asks.
Whatever.

A Message To People Pleasers

Oh people pleasers!
Why don't you please the purpose for why you were created?
Why don't you please the energies that formed you?
Why don't you please the wisdoms that guide you?
You walk around and make decisions with concern about what others think,
when instead you can focus on how the Beloved would feel.
Forget about what others do.
Ask what Love would do.
And then let Love do.

Climb like a lion.
You were not born to be a sheep amongst a fenced herd.
Your soul is a shepherd.
Allow yourself to be guided.
Remarkable happenings are destined when you do.
Every moment,
your past experiences,
your future dreams,
is shaping you for why you've been made.
Do not get lost in pleasing others,
or in proving others wrong.
Both are childish acts.
The only thing you must please is this purpose.
Please the energies that made you,
that made life,
by being relentlessly true and coherent with the unique nature of your soul.

Love Has Made Me A Madman

Love has ripped the sheets over my eyes and taken me by the heart.
Love has trampled through my mind and flooded my thoughts with its perfume.
Love has transformed my feet into lips upon which I kiss the earth everywhere I step.
Love has fermented my mind into wine.
My soul is a tavern,
eager to welcome drunkards home.

All I can speak is this poetry.
The rest of the time I'm mesmerized.
My being sings of rapture.
My soul is Love's candle.
The Flame that's kindled us never diminishes.
To share the light is to share the love.
Love has made me a madman on a mission to brighten up humanity.

Between Future And Past

I stand between two realms:
future and past.

Everything behind me has shaped me,
molded me,
prepared me,
blessed me,
for what is here,
and what is to come.

Everything ahead of me has called me,
drawn me,
pulled me,
hungered me,
for what I must do,
and who I must become.

The future has blessed the past with meaning,
and the past has blessed the future with destiny.
But where have these blessings come from?

Within the stream of Now
these two dimensions blend like honey and milk
as we are taken into the depths of the ocean of eternity.
Timelessness.
Spaciousness.
Emptiness.
Infiniteness.

These are the waves we ride.
From here,
all possibilities emerge.
From here,
we can see a new world emerge from Love.

Don't get lost in this world you call real.
In a moment of pure observation,
what you thought was so solid transforms.
Use this gift of focus wisely.
Don't waste it on anything other than magnifying the miraculous nature
of life.

The Visionary

The visionary lives in their vision
and brings it into the world by their way of being.
All their doings are fueled
by their passionate obsession to create.
They commit themselves soul-fully
to this passionate way of being,
as a creative alchemist,
where they know their every action, thought, feeling, and intention
is an opportunity to bring forth more richness.
This way of life is home for them.
To be a passenger in life is not an option.

Consciousness.
Intentionality.
Purpose.
Passion.
This is their way of being.

They know life is a dream.
They seek the Dreamer,
and in their seeking,
they become one with dream,
dreaming,
and Dreamer.

From these intersecting,
interdependent,
interrelated fields,
they create.

The Lover's Insanity

Your Glance has made me ravenous.
My hunger for You is beyond desire and lust.
I've become insane and now see you everywhere,
in everything.

This insanity is the passionate frenzy of lovers.
Love's intoxication opens their inner eye,
and they see their Beloved everywhere.
Only with heart fully embracing
can one be granted such potent wine.

What Are You Seeking?

Oh soul,
What do you seek with such ferocity?
What's at the root of your burning desire?
Growth is natural.
Joy is natural.
Adventure is natural.
Wisdom is natural.
Synchronicity is natural.
Purpose is natural.
Miracles are natural.
Gifts are natural.
Giving is natural.
Receiving is natural.
Life is natural.
Love is natural.
You are natural.
We are natural.
From Nature, we are.
Nature, we are.
Open the treasure chest of the Infinite
by seeking the roots of your very beingness.

Because It Was You

Because it was You who planted this dream in my heart,
I am relentless in its total pursuit.

Oh Soul of souls,
Take the steering wheel of my heart and guide it wherever you wish.
This Light you've invested in me is meant to be shared.
Use me as a lighthouse of Your Passion,
bringing souls Home,
and bringing Home to everywhere.

Soul Has Taken Me

Soul has taken me out from the cityscape of thoughts
and into a realm between places and spaciousness,
existence and non-existence.
Soul has flooded me with purpose
like mountain springs bringing about new life.
Soul has whispered the love story of creation
into the depths of my being.
Soul has made me into a lover of mysteries,
reading the tablets, volumes, and scrolls of wisdom
from the eyes of all beings.

Love Is Wild

Love does not come gently like a morning breeze.
Love is not comfortable.
Love comes with an explosion,
from the inside.
Love takes you out of the shell you once called yourself.
Love is wild, drunk, and rampant on destroying all that is not authentic.
Love does not care about trophies and accolades.
Love rips apart all that you treasured and humiliates you into humility.
Only then do you recognize the true treasures that live within all of us.
When Love comes for you,
do not hide.
Do not hold yourself strong,
acting as if you've got yourself all together.
Let yourself fall,
and in that falling,
you're given wings.

Nectar Of Life

I have lost my appetite for reason and knowledge.
My ravenous hunger only wants more of this Sweetness that unifies all of creation together so perfectly.

Oh Nectar of life,
Take me into the Honeycomb.
Make me your prisoner.
I'm Your servant bee,
wildly buzzing in the field of Love,
enraptured in sharing this Honey with all.

The Roof Has Collapsed From Within

O lovers, mystics, caravaners of Joy!
Rejoice! Rejoice!
The roof has collapsed from within
and down with it has come all logic and reason!
I have lost my mind in Your Love.
All thoughts have flown away
and returned to me as love poems
that dance like dust motes
around Your Beacon of Love.
I have become ecstatic music
singing for Your Sweet Essence.

Once a dreamer,
I now only long to be Your Dream.
I wander an open field
surrounded by the sweetness of roses,
none so sweet as The One
that has made me a drunkard,
this perfume of Love's Heart
that tantalizes my entire being
like the Sun that warms the entire world
into the passionate expression of Life.

Who Is It That Seeks Within My Seeking?

Who is it that seeks within my seeking?
Who is it that feels within my feeling?
Who is it that sees within my seeing?
Who is it that observes within my observing?
Who is it that animates my animating?
Who is this soul,
and where did it come from?
I intend to find out.

Burning In Love

I am burning in the furnace of Love.
All my thoughts have become flames of passion.
Language and reason has left the door of mind
and taken me with them.
I've heard the myths of alchemists
who've transmuted lead into gold.
This Love has transformed my lead-mind
into a soliloquy of tormenting rapture.
The agonizing nectar of longing has driven me mad.
I have become a hollow canoe,
floating amongst Love's ocean,
aching for a shipwreck.

In all I see,
all I do,
all I feel,
my Beloved is here,
and yet I ache for more.

Intimacy is a portal with no end.
Passionate drunkards can't experience enough.
They're obsessed.
Even in their dreams,
They sink deeper and deeper in love.

Lion Of Love

Dear souls,
Wake up!
Wake up!
Wake up!
You are Infinite!
You are Consciousness!
You are Love!
Quit seeking the opinions of others.
Know for yourself.
Go out and live.
You are the Origin of the origin.

Be a lion of Love,
Stand tall with your chest up,
your heart expanded,
and your pride for the Love that made you.
Know your nature and be one with it.

Come, Come, My Dear Heart

Come, come, my dear heart.
Come out of your cave and into the world.
Every corner has a new adventure.
Every turn brings you towards a new destiny.
Follow your inner guidance always
and know that the inner is meant to bring you outer.
There are many fools in this world,
but to be a fool is to fool oneself.
Your soul will never fool you.
Your soul always knows what's needed
for the fulfillment of your incarnation.
Come, come, explore with your whole soul.

Witness As A Lover

To witness is to become one with.
It is an act of consciousness.
Witnessing the beauty, marvel, awe, and miraculous nature
of another, of the sky, of the ocean, of the sunset,
awakens us to the truth
of our interconnectedness and oneness as Life.

Lovers are wondrous witnesses.
They are lit up by seeing the Love that has crafted all form.
This Light they observe in all life is the wine of the soul.

Lovers are drunkards.
They are constantly drinking this wine
and also being fermented as it.
Lovers see every exchange,
every interaction,
as a love story of souls coming together on-purpose,
gifting one another with a particular energy
necessary for their destinies and for life's destiny.

Lovers are passionate witnesses.
Their passionate witnessing is intoxicatingly liberating.
It is what gives another human being wings
so they can fly as the soul that they are.

Bear witness to the Love that creates, guides,
and brings all together.
Synchronicity is true happening.

Love's Passion To Serve

In the center of the Universe,
I spin in drunken praise.
Glory is everywhere.
Like a river flowing,
Love moves me
into the Ocean of God.
Like a grain of salt dissolving,
I vanish in the Heart of Divinity.
Like counting prayer beads,
I praise You over and over.
How can I bless the Blesser?
How can I give to the Giver?

Love,
take me in Your Heart.
Let me serve,
however,
be it sweeping floors
or greeting guests.

Explore With Passion

There is a whole world to explore,
dear soul.
There is an adventure that lies beyond every corner.
All outward journeys bring you deeper inwards.
All inward journeys bring more of you outwards.
Wherever you begin,
keep on exploring with passion.

Take a detour.
Embark on new adventures.
Pause.
Take in the moment.
Bless out your beingness.
Life is not a race.
Fulfillment of your soul's purpose is what's most important,
and a detour may be what gets you back on track.

Drunk In My Longing

I've become drunk in my longing,
dizzy for so many days.
Where can I find more of this Love?
A Voice answers,
"Find Me in the novelty
of this moment and the next."

Blessed By The Burning Of Love

We are all pieces
of the Whole,
belonging to the Whole.
We are luminous beings
lit alive by the same Light.
When you see a dim candle,
bless it with your flame…
Your Source will never extinguish,
only expand,
as more are blessed by your burning with Love.

Remembering And Forgetting

Sometimes remembering can be a curse
and forgetfulness can be a useful attribute.
Have you not grown tired
of remembering all that you perceive
went wrong in your life?
What if you forgot
all the self-perpetuating lies,
these mentally rehearsed illusions?
What if you forgot
all the painful memorization,
those selected pieces
that lack full-dimensionality,
that burn you with inner-acids
like anger, regret, and pity?

Dear soul!
Choose to remember all that's true.
Choose to forget all that's illusion.
Drink the Beloved's wine
and let your memories become Love-stained.
The only memories that should haunt you are those that bring your
heart into deeper longing for God: Love's hangover.

Rubab Of Joy

A man was walking down a street full of vendors
selling fresh naan, dried fruits, seasonal vegetables,
and a variety of spices.
He was joyfully playing a rubab
with the zest for life bouncing in his every step
and the kind of smile the Sun gives to the land
every morning it turns its face towards a new dawn.

Lovers are passionate beings.
They crave sharing the Light with all
with their full beingness.

Afterlife

This poem is dedicated to my aunt Bereshkai
who showed me that true power is gentle, kind, giving, and loving.

You took one last breath
and my whole Universe fell silent.
The galaxies stopped spinning
to gaze upon your beautiful face,
shimmering tears of grief-filled goodbyes.
The wind stopped blowing
and the ocean sat still.
The crickets stopped chirping
as the emotions began to spill.

How could Life take this angel away who,
even in their final moments,
could only think and do what blessings would,
care-taking for all others…
when all others wished to care for her?

What kind of heart gives always and freely
until its last beat?
What kind of love nurtures always and freely
even while enduring so much pain?

Your passing was a tragedy to us all,
but you said,
"Don't cry.
I'm not leaving you.

I'm embarking on a new adventure,
one where I can be with and love all of you,
all the time,
from the landless land of timelessness.
A seed descends under the Earth and rises a tree.
Like this I will bring more love for you all.
Never think I've left you.
I breathe in you with the essence of Love."

You gave us one last kiss with your soul
and then became more than human ever could.
You transitioned to the spacious, spaceless space,
the field of Eternal Love,
from where I feel your watching and guiding,
beyond and within my heart.
Once embodied Love,
You are now Eternal Love.
Once human melody,
You are now the Heart's Song.

Bonus Verses

There's a prayer unique to lovers
who long for the Beloved
with such passionate intensity.
Their life is prayer
praying for just one glance from the Beloved.

Focus on Love
and miracles will follow.

I've become drunk in my longing,
dizzy for so many days.
Where can I find more of this Love?
A voice answers,
"Find me in the novelty
of this moment and the next."

There is a sacred dance
between Oneness
and uniqueness.
The Ocean links all life within it together.
Within the Ocean

is it's perplexities.
How can there be
any spice in life,
any color,
without uniqueness and diversity?

Nature gives a rainforest
a full spectrum of life
in vast variety of forms and colors.
The Cosmos contains more stars
than there is life on planet Earth.
Each star unique
and part of the whole.
Oh God!
Oh God!
Oh God!
This is all I can say
in mesmerized awe.

God is everywhere
and in every here.
Lovers passionately seek
the novelty of every moment.
They speak "ooooos and ahhhhhs"
through their wonder-filled eyes.

Oh God!
This glorious gap
from unknown to manifest!
The humility in feeling so insignificant
and knowing all is Your Blessing!

Oh God!
Please fill this gap,
with Your Ever-Flowing Love!
Even with an ounce of Your Love!
I will carry it in my soul,
kissed by the Balm of Eternity.

Never can I be-lie-ve,
be-with-this-lie-and-live,
that I am separate from others.
Never can I believe
that I am separate from You!
Only knowing.
Only realizing.
Real-eyes-ing.

I live in You,
You live in me.
This is the relationship
of lover and Beloved.
Your Love is balm
to this separate,
fractured,
wounded ego-self!

Oh God!
How you connect us,
How you inter-direct us,
How you mix us!
Your Presence is found
in the space between
they and me.
Your Love is glue
unifying us souls.

Oh God!
I would give my life
to live in this space
where you glue from.

There is a sacred timing
that orchestrates our life
like an ever-flowing map.
X marks the Heart.
Destiny calls to the sleepless soul
who cannot settle any longer,
who cannot live this illusion,
who cannot submit to ordinary.

There's an Effortless Current
that moves all life
through joyous,
inclusive,
wholesome,
evolution.

Oh how effortless
we all manifest.

I'm so drunk,
I've lost my way
to anywhere.
Guide me
like a shepherd
into Your Depths.

There is an awareness
that's omnipresent with Love.
There is a Righteousness
more righteous than all those amongst us.
I've awoken in a realm
between dream and reality.
This meta-love pulsates around
the enveloping,
expansive,
field of light and sound
that is "me".

This slap comes from no hand
and wakes one up to new waking.
The lover is blessed by all doings.
This scolding is tbe end of sleepwalking,
Love's Slap to new waking.

Oh Love!
I'm in love with the Love
of which all love yearns for.

You are the Mystic Whisperer.
We are your love-whispers.
You are the Majestic Dreamer.
We are your dreams manifesting.

There is a magnetic pull
between desire and desirer.
The mystic craves the foodless food
and tracks it with his sense for the senseless.

Oh Grace!
You've caught me stumbling
and carried me into this blissful flight.
Where is it that I end and You begin?
Beyond the reach of my fingertips,
I feel You,
and within that,
I feel myself.
Within the center of myself,
I can feel your warming presence,
like a hearth that all of me gathers around.

I've traveled through the sands of time,
seen the many winds of change,
heard the sweet songs of grace,
swam the depths of the sea of love,
all within a moment-less moment of silent prayer.

Oh Weaver of Love!
You magically guide,
direct,
introduce,
and bless all into magical union
with sacred purpose.
All chance meetings are Your Orchestration.
All coincidences were Your Planning.

Gratitude is the sweet delicacy
that souls give to one another.
This euphoric sweetness takes us beyond our senses
to the realm of the Beloved's Passion.

There is a special joy found in traveling.
To wander this earthly plane
and look at all things with wonder.

Oh God!
Teach me the secret
to living consciously.

Dear soul,
Live with ever-wakefulness.
Pinch yourself regularly.
Know this is a dream
and you can dream something better
for everybody.

Oh God!
Teach me the secret
to living abundantly.

Dear soul,
Be a bringer of the abundance
that you wish to reap.
Sow those seeds with love and generosity.
Water them with presence.
Place all faith
in this nurturing river of synchronicity.
See every step you take
as an adventure into the Tavern of Love.
Drink yourself full until all you can see
is life through this lens of intoxicating passion.
Be a generator of generosity.
What goes around comes back around, tenfold,
and beyond,
for all.

Oh God!
Teach me the secret
to living lovingly.

Dear soul,
See all as Love
existing within My Heart.

Oh Love!
Your Presence is pervasive throughout my life.
Ever since my love-barreled-heart has flowed open,
I've been left with this hangover.
You let the barrels flow with Your Wine
and I became the drunkard's prayer.
I've awoken now and can hardly stand.
I'm intoxicated by this hangover of passionate remembrance.
Every atom of my being
vibrates with ecstasy.
My heart sings,
"Let the wine-barrels flow!
No one will be left thirsty!
My source is Infinite!
All may drank from my loving!"

Oh God!
You've given me Love
and I ache to share it.

Lovers are passionate gardeners of joy.
They relish every moment as an honor
to plant more Love in the heart-gardens of all.
They treasure every moment as a joy
to pour more wine into the heart-glasses
of all they meet.

Oh soul!
You are not meant to be sleepwalking
In an illusory state of existence.
You are a being of Love.
Wake up in your wakefulness.
Dream in your sleepfulness.
Wake up to your beingness.

Praise be to those souls
who through one impression they make,
new blessed destinies are unfolded.

The caravan of lovers has arrived.
Joy fills the streets.
Love fills the air.
Music fills the hearts.
Stars are smiling with glimmering radiance.
Miracles are unfolding one smile at a time.
Rejoice in the celebration of life.
Marvel at the Magic that created all of this.

Without sweetness
baklava is empty.
Without soul
body is empty.
Without being

human is empty.
Without Love
heart is beat-less.

For the love of Love,
I have given myself wholeheartedly,
like the rose who opens for the honey bee.
Look at the marvelous nature
of nature itself.
You see the mulberry seed
birth a mulberry tree.
This tree provides abundant fruit
for many beings
and the only leaves that silkworms will eat.
They go on to make adorned tapestries
containing the signature of the tree,
which contains the signature of the seed,
which contains the signature of the fruit,
which is all inscribed with Love.

Lovers are bold like a lion,
ever-present with their focus,
entirely fixated on their Beloved.
You were not made to be
a pawn of someone else's game,
nor to be conditioned
within someone else's expectations.
Awaken the lion of Love.

What is the ocean?
A collection of water droplets?
None are separate.
All form the ocean.
All are the interconnected ocean.
We are the interconnected Ocean of Love.
Beloved's Heart is the Ocean.
Our hearts,
an ocean within the Ocean,
and the Ocean within an ocean.

Love has awoken me of my-self.
I'm now a river of Love's blessings.
Boundless,
timeless,
interconnected,
interwoven,
I see and feel You.
You've opened me to see and know
the interconnected Love we all are.

I pause from this endless searching
and sink between dimensions into eternity.
Oh the sacred gift
to be Infinite Consciousness,
to experience vast diversity,
to be fully alive,
to be part of this Sea of Infinity!

Do not cower behind yourself.
You are infinity focalized into a being.
Oh Lion of Love!
If I'm lucky,
may Your Gaze land upon me!

In the midst of all this noise,
chaos's seemingly never-ending screams for attention,
there is one noise that calls me
with the screams of rapture.
Drown in this endless chasm of silence,
where chaos and order co-exist,
where instability and stability dance together,
were existence and non-existence intertwine.
Live between the raindrops.

Close those two eyes of yours
so you can clearly see with your inner eyes,
the intuitive eyes that simply know.

I am but a blade of grass
in the Garden of Your Heart.

Praise to Love
for all the friendships its forged,
for all the lovers its liberated,
for all the joys its freed.

My burning love is so intense,
it can boil the sea into steam.
My heart is dancing in all directions.

I am a fabric of joy,
sewn into the Quilt of Eternity
by Sacred Hands.
I am so one with you,
I've melted with you and become Love's Chocolate.

I am a Rubab.
Love is the tone
that my every fiber has been entrained to.

I am a rock thrown into Your Ocean,
sinking into Love's Infinite Embrace.
My ripples echo with ecstasy and praise.
Love is my Master.

Patience knows that it takes energy
to go from a seed to a seedling,
from a sprout to a tree.

Only the spiritually blind fall in love
with plastic toys and stone trinkets
that have a name branded on them,
like cattle branded by a stable master.
Your soul has been branded by Infinite Wisdoms.
Love has set you free from the mind's stable.

Be in this silence
and you'll be taken to the place
of infinite spaciousness,
of infinite possibility,
beyond senses,
beyond mind,
where you become tensionless.
Lost,
in the middle of the desert,
thirsty and without water,
I am pulled in Your Direction.

I am a visitor
between this world
and the next.
I live between dimensions.
My home is Love's Heart.
Self,
Other,
You,

Me,
All colors on the rainbow,
reflecting both Creation's Collective Prism
and Divinity's Unique Expression.

Dear soul!
Your name is beyond words,
spoken by Love.

www.ingramcontent.com/pod-product-compliance
Lightning Source LLC
Chambersburg PA
CBHW030328100526
44592CB00010B/607